Notting Hill Editions is an independent British publisher. The company was founded by Tom Kremer (1930–2017), champion of innovation and the man responsible for popularising the Rubik's Cube.

After a successful business career in toy invention Tom decided, at the age of eighty, to fulfil his passion for literature. In a fast-moving digital world Tom's aim was to revive the art of the essay, and to create exceptionally beautiful books that would be cherished.

Hailed as 'the shape of things to come', the family-run press brings to print the most surprising thinkers of past and present. In an era of information-overload, these collectible pocket-size books distil ideas that linger in the mind.

Julian Barnes is the author of thirteen novels including *The Sense of an Ending*, which won the 2011 Booker Prize, and *Sunday Times* bestsellers *The Noise of Time* and *The Only Story*. He has also written three books of short stories, four collections of essays and three books of non-fiction, including the *Sunday Times* number-one bestseller *Levels of Life* and *Nothing to be Frightened of*. In 2017 he was awarded the Légion d'honneur.

CHANGING MY MIND

—

Julian Barnes

nh Notting Hill Editions

Published in 2025
by Notting Hill Editions Ltd
Mirefoot, Burneside, Kendal LA8 9AB

Series and cover design by Tom Etherington

Typeset by CB Editions, London
Printed and bound in Great Britain by Clays Ltd, St Ives plc

Versions of these essays were first broadcast on BBC Radio 3's
The Essay series in 2016.

A CIP record for this book is available from the British Library

ISBN 978-1-912559-69-5

nottinghilleditions.com

Contents

– Memories –

It sounds a simple business. 'I changed my mind.' Subject, verb, object – a clear, clean action, without correcting or diminishing adjectives or adverbs. 'No, I'm not doing that – I changed my mind' is usually an irrefutable statement. It implies the presence of strong arguments which can be provided if necessary. The economist John Maynard Keynes, charged with inconsistency, famously replied, 'When the facts change, I change my mind.' So, he – and we – are happily and confidently in charge of this whole operation. The world may sadly incline to inconsistency, but not us.

And yet the phrase covers a great variety of mental activities, some seemingly rational and logical, others elemental and instinctive. There may be a simmering-away beneath the level of consciousness until the bursting realisation comes that, yes, you have changed your mind completely on this subject, that person, this theory, that world view. The Dadaist Francis Picabia once put it like this:

1

'Our heads are round so that our thoughts can change direction.' And I think this feels as close to a true accounting of our mental processes as does Maynard Keynes's statement.

When I was growing up, adults of my parents' generation used to say, 'Changing her mind is a woman's privilege.' This was, according to your male point of view, either a charming or an infuriating characteristic. It was regarded as something essentially female, or feminine, sometimes mere whimsicality, sometimes deeply emotional and intuitively intelligent – again, intuition was back then a female speciality – and related to the very nature of the woman in question. So perhaps you could say men were Keynesian, and women Picabian.

You rarely hear that phrase about a woman's privilege nowadays, and to many it sounds doubtless merely sexist and patronising. On the other hand, if you approach the matter from a philosophical or neuroscientific point of view, it looks a little different. 'I changed my mind.' Subject, verb, object, a simple transaction under our control. But where is this 'I' that is changing this 'mind', like some rider controlling a horse with their knees, or the driver of a tank guiding its progress? Certainly not very visible to the eye of the philosopher or brain scientist. This 'I' we feel so confident about isn't something beyond and separate from the mind, controlling it, but rather something inside the mind, and arising from it. In the words of one neuroscientist, 'there is no self-stuff' locatable within the brain. Far from being a horse-rider or tank-commander, we are at the wheel of a driver-less car of the near future. To the outside observer, there is a car, and a steering wheel, with someone sitting in front of it. And this is true – except that on this particular model the driver cannot switch from automatic to manual, because manual does not exist.

So if things are this way round – if it's the brain, the mind that gives birth to what we think of as 'I', then the phrase 'I changed my mind' doesn't make much sense. You might as well say, 'My mind changed me.' And if we see things this way round, then changing one's mind is something we don't necessarily understand ourselves. In which case, it's not just a woman's privilege, but a human privilege. Though perhaps 'privilege' isn't quite the right word – better to say, characteristic, or oddity.

Sometimes in my life, I've been a logical Keynesian about the whole business, sometimes a Dadaist Picabian. But generally, in either case, I've been confident that I was right to change my mind. This is another characteristic of the process. We never think, Oh, I've changed my mind and have now adopted a weaker or less plausible view than the one I held before, or a sillier or more sentimental view. We always believe that changing our mind is an improvement, bringing a greater truthfulness, or a greater sense of realism, to our dealings with the world and other people. It puts an end to vacillation, uncertainty, weak-mindedness. It seems to make us stronger and more mature; we have put away yet another childish thing. Well, we would think that, wouldn't we?

I remember the story of an Oxford undergraduate of literary aspirations visiting Garsington Manor in the 1920s where the artistic hostess Lady Ottoline Morrell presided. She asked him, 'Do you prefer spring or autumn, young man?' He replied spring. Her riposte was that when he got older he would probably prefer autumn. In the late 1970s I interviewed the novelist William Gerhardie, who was almost exactly half a century older than me. I was young and callow, he was extremely aged, indeed bed-ridden. He asked me if I believed in the afterlife. I said that I didn't. 'Well, you might when you get to my age,' he replied with a chuckle.

I admired him for the remark, while not believing that I would ever change my mind to that degree.

But we all expect, indeed approve of, some changes over the years. We change our minds about many things, from matters of mere taste – the colours we prefer, the clothes we wear – to aesthetic matters – the music, the books we like – to adherence to social groups – the football team or political party we support – to the highest verities – the person we love, the God we revere, the significance or insignificance of our place in the seemingly empty or mysteriously full universe. We make these decisions – or these decisions make us – constantly, though they are often camouflaged by the momentousness of the acts that provoke them. Love, parenthood, the death of those close to us: such matters reorient our lives, and often make us change our minds. Is it merely that the facts have changed? No, it's more that areas of fact and feeling hitherto unknown to us have suddenly become clear, that the emotional landscape has altered. And in a great swirl of emotion, our minds change. So I think, on the whole, I have become a Picabian rather than a Keynesian.

Consider the question of memory. This is often a key factor in changing our mind: we need to forget what we believed before, or at least forget with what passion and certainty we believed it, because we now believe something different that we know to be truer and deeper. Memory, or the weakening or lack of it, helps endorse our new position; it is part of the process. And beyond this, there's the wider question of how our understanding of memory changes. Mine certainly has over my lifetime. When I was an unreflecting boy, I assumed that memory operated like a left-luggage office. An event in our lives happens, we make some swift, subconscious judgement on the importance of that event, and if it is important enough, we store it in our memory. Later, when we need to recall it, we take the left-luggage ticket along to a department of our brain, which releases the memory back to us – and there it is, as fresh and uncreased as the moment it happened.

But we know it's not like that really. We know that memory degrades. We have come to understand that every time we take that memory out of the locker and expose it to view, we make some tiny alteration to it. And so the stories we tell most often about our lives are likely to be the least reliable, because we will have subtly amended them in every retelling down the years.

Sometimes it doesn't take years at all. I have an

old friend, a considerable raconteur, who once, in my presence, in the course of a single day, told the same anecdote to three different audiences with three different punchlines. At the third hearing, after the laughter had subsided, I murmured, perhaps a little unkindly, 'Wrong ending, Thomas.' He looked at me in disbelief (at my manners); I looked at him in disbelief (at his not being able to stick to a reliable narrative).

There is also such a thing as a memory transplant. My wife and I were great friends of the painter Howard Hodgkin, and travelled with him and his partner to many places. In 1989, we were in Taranto in southern Italy, when Howard spotted a black towel in an old-fashioned haberdasher's window. We went in, Howard asked to see it, and the assistant produced from a drawer a black towel. No, Howard explained, it wasn't quite the same black as the one in the window. The assistant, unflustered, produced another one, and then another one, each of which Howard rejected as not being as black as the one in the window. After he had turned down seven or eight, I was thinking (as one might), for God's sake, it's only a towel, you only need it to dry your face. Then Howard asked the assistant to get the one out of the window, and we all saw at once that it was indeed very, very slightly blacker than all the others. A sale was concluded, and a lesson about the precision of an artist's eye learned. I described this incident in an essay about Howard, and doubtless told it orally a few times as well. Many years later, after Howard's death, I was at dinner in painterly circles when a woman, addressing her husband, said, 'Do you remember when we went into that shop with Howard for a black towel . . . ' Before she could finish, I reminded her firmly that this was *my* story, which her expression clearly acknowledged. And I don't believe she was doing it knowingly: she somehow remembered it as happening to her and her husband. It was an artless borrowing – or a piece of mental cannibalism, if you prefer.

It's salutary to discover, from time to time, how other people's memories are often quite different from our own – not just of events, but of what we ourselves were like back then. A few years ago, I had an exchange of correspondence about one of my books with someone whom I'd been at school with, but had not kept up with and had no memory of. The exchange turned into a sharp disagreement, at which point he clearly decided he might as well tell me what he thought of me – or, more accurately, tell me what he remembered now of what he had thought of me back when we were at school together. 'I remember you,' he wrote, 'as a noisy and irritating presence in the Sixth Form corridor.' This came as a great surprise to me, and I had to laugh, if a little ruefully. My own memory insisted – and still does – that I was a shy, self-conscious and well-behaved boy, though inwardly rebellious. But I couldn't deny this fellow-pupil's reminiscence; and so, belatedly, I factored it in, and changed my mind about what I must have been like – or, at least, how I might have appeared to others – fifty and more years ago.

Gradually, I have come to change my mind about the very nature of memory itself. For a long time I stuck pretty much with the left-luggage-department theory, presuming that some people's memories were better because their brain's storage conditions were better, or they had shaped and lacquered their memories better before depositing them in the first place. Some years ago, I was writing a book which was mainly about death, but also a family memoir. I have one brother – three years older, a philosopher by profession – and emailed him explaining what I was up to. I asked some preliminary questions about our parents – how he judged them as parents, what they had taught us, what he thought their own relationship was like. I added that he himself would inevitably feature in my book. He replied with an initial declaration that astonished me. 'By the way,' he wrote, 'I don't mind what you say about me, and if your memory conflicts with mine, go with yours, as it is probably better.' I thought this was not just extremely generous of him, but also very interesting. Though he was only three years older than me, he was assuming the superiority of my memory. I guessed that this could be because he was a philosopher, living in a world of higher and more theoretical ideas; whereas I was a novelist, professionally up to my neck in the scruffy, everyday details of life.

But it was more than this. As he explained to me, he had come to distrust memory as a guide to the past. By itself, unsubstantiated, uncorroborated memory was in his view no better than an act of the imagination. (James Joyce put it the other way round, 'Imagination is memory' – which is much more dubious.) My brother gave an example. In 1976 he had gone to a philosophical conference on Stoic logic held at Chantilly, north of Paris, organised by Jacques Brunschwig, whom he had never met before. He took a train from Boulogne, and clearly remembered missing his stop, and having to take a taxi back up the line and arriving late as a consequence. He and Brunschwig became close friends, and thirty years later they were having dinner in Paris and reminiscing about how they first met. Brunschwig remembered how he had waited on the platform at Chantilly and immediately recognised my brother as soon as he stepped down from the train. They stared at one another in disbelief (and perhaps had to apply some Stoic logic to their quandary).

That book came out fifteen years ago. And in the meantime, I have come round to my brother's point of view. I now agree that memory, a single person's memory, uncorroborated and unsubstantiated by other evidence, is a feeble guide to the past. I think, more strongly than I used to, that we constantly reinvent our lives, retelling them – usually – to our own advantage. I believe that the operation of memory is closer to an act of the imagination than it is to the clean and reliably detailed recuperation of an event in our past. I think that sometimes we remember as true things which never even happened in the first place; that we may grossly embellish an original incident out of all recognition; that we may cannibalise someone else's memory, and change not just the endings of the stories of our lives, but also their middles and beginnings. I think that memory, over time, changes, and, indeed, changes our mind. That's what I believe at the moment, anyway. Though in a few years, perhaps I will have changed my mind about it all over again.

– Words –

I've spent my life with words, writing them and reading them. Words are how I construct my picture of the world out there – both the real one I live in, and the fictional ones I create. I begin my day reading words in a printed newspaper, and end it before turning out the light with a magazine or book. I believe deeply in words, in their ability to represent thought, define truth and create beauty. I'm equally aware that words are constantly used for the opposite purposes: to obfuscate truth, misrepresent thought, lie, slander and provoke hatred. I also think of words as being mobile, slippery, metamorphic.

When I was a boy, playing some word-game with my family, any altercations would be answered with a cry of, 'Look it up in the dictionary!' There were two parts to this looking-up: the first related to the word's status, indeed existence: if a word wasn't in the dictionary, then it didn't, in any real sense, exist. 'Not in the dictionary!' was a triumphant result for an opponent. The second part was to do with meaning: a word meant what the dictionary said it meant, nothing more, nothing less. The dictionary in question was a Chambers, so a moderately hefty but still single-volume work. And I childishly assumed that such a dictionary contained all the words that existed – or at least, that did or would exist for practical purposes in my life.

Adolescence, and the awareness of sex, made me realize that there were more words in heaven and earth than were dreamt of in the dictionary. I remember, in idle moments, looking up words and phrases I suspected had something to do with sex; also, the new words and phrases boys used with a sense of thrilled discovery. That they 'weren't in the dictionary' and couldn't be employed in front of my parents, made them, of course, all the more thrilling to use in private.

But I still believed in the overall authority of the dictionary, and while not much given to philosophical reflection, I assumed two things about words, their life and their history. The first was that words matched the world: that every word stood for a real something out there; and conversely, that everything out there in the world had its appropriate name, and that name, that word, was to be found in the dictionary. And the second thing I quasi-assumed was that at the moment when a thing was named – whether by Adam in the Garden of Eden, or some lexically-advanced caveman – the word meant nothing other than the thing denoted by it. So – in other words – there was a golden age, a peaceable kingdom in which all the words lay down happily with one another, meaning no more and no less than they did, and blissfully attached each to its own single thing, idea, item, notion.

Put like this, it sounds a bit absurd – deliberately so. But it is, I think, the belief most of us start off having about words, and some continue on with: the notion that words have some fixed, original, authentic meaning, and that the only way to go thereafter is down. This lexical golden-ageism often joins hands with grammatical prescriptivism – never end a sentence with a preposition, never split an infinitive, and so on – to create many mournful and irritated letters to the newspapers about the decline of language and, with it, civilisation. Once you can't trust a word to mean what it 'always has', then the world starts to go to hell in a handbasket, as my mother used to say. Though that's an odd word for a start – handbasket. And how might the world go to hell in one?

I began to realise that there was something

wrong with such linguistic absolutism when I got my first job after university: as an editorial assistant on a new supplement to the Oxford English Dictionary. I spent three years researching the history of certain words and phrases between B and G, trying to find their earliest printed use, writing etymologies, pronunciations and definitions. It was very particular, microscopic work – I remember spending days reading through books on cricket, trying to find the earliest printed use of the word 'gully' – but those three years changed most of my previous assumptions about words – and dictionaries.

If I went in as an unthinking conservative prescriptivist, I came out a liberal descriptivist. I no longer believed in some Golden Age of language, some platonic matching of word and thing. Nor did I accept the myth of linguistic decline – that once upon a time language was employed by people who always knew their wrist from their elbow, until the barbarians came through the gates bringing misuse, inaccuracy, vulgarisation. I came to believe instead that language was – and is – often approximate, that words mean only what we generally agree that they mean, and that the English language has always been in a state of tumultuous motion – and all the better for it.

Let me give a couple of examples. When the Welsh Labour politician Ray Gunter resigned from parliament in 1972, he made an emotional speech in which he said he was going back to the valleys 'from whence I have come'. There was a certain amount of mockery – posh mockery – of Gunter for this remark. Ho ho, he doesn't know that 'whence' means 'from where', so 'from whence' is like saying 'from from where', good riddance to this linguistic oaf. But – look it up in the dictionary – 'from whence' is well attested in both Shakespeare and the Bible (Gunter was doubtless referencing Psalm 121: 'I will lift up mine eyes unto the hills, from whence cometh my help'). Grammarians who try to impose grammar on a moving language, to force it backwards into some false original purity of structure, are always on to a loser. Still, at least – and this is not something I say very often – at least we are not French. For centuries the French had – and still have – the Académie Française sitting in judgment on what is truly and authentically a French word, and finding 'proper' alternatives for unacceptable neologisms and imports, like 'le weekend'. Needless to say, their deliberations have long since been irrelevant to the way the French speak, and write. A few years ago a French professor told me of an acquaintance of hers, a snobbish young Parisian, who introduced his companion as '*my friend*' with a full French accent, of course.

My second example concerns the words 'uninterested' and 'disinterested'. These are often cited as an example of how two decent words with distinctive meanings have become confused through sloppy usage. According to this widely held notion, 'uninterested' means 'not interested', and 'disinterested' means 'impartial'. To do something uninterestedly is quite different from doing it disinterestedly. But then the aforesaid linguistic oafs started using 'disinterested' to mean 'uninterested', the original, true sense of 'disinterested' became lost, and we're now all going to hell in that handbasket, or sometimes handcart. I have an instinctive sympathy for this complaint – I would much prefer these two words to be distinguishable in meaning – but if you look at the historical evidence, the story is far less clear. The first use of 'uninterested' in the OED is in the sense of 'disinterested', and the first use of the word 'disinterested' is in the sense of 'uninterested'. Instead of the myth of decline, we find the truth of centuries-long muddle.

When, shortly after my dictionary years, I started writing fiction, I took these beliefs about language with me. The English language is – has always been – a mongrel beast: that is partly where its vigour, energy and suppleness come from. Its porosity to the languages and dialects of other English-speaking countries acts as a regular blood transfusion. Any writer born into the English language is very lucky: not just for all the many potential readers out there, but for the very words he or she is given to play – to play seriously – with.

Of course, being a liberal relativist about words doesn't mean that I think anyone can use the language – written or spoken – as well as anyone else. The war against cliché is ongoing – even if, as I write it, that phrase – the war against cliché – sounds, well, a bit of a cliché. Obviously, some writers are better than others – in clarity, style, expressiveness, effect. Obviously, a writer shouldn't needlessly confuse a reader, only needfully – for a specific and well-understood purpose. Obviously, the bad linguistic guys are still out there – seeking our vote, trying to sell us a product, lying to us about what happened – by bad or misleading use of language. And yet I believe that in the end good language drives out bad, and that the obfuscators will be defeated, partly by the very strength of language itself.

At the same time, just as I celebrate the endless malleability of the language I use to write in, there are changes I don't like. Within the tolerant former lexicographer lies the grumpy older citizen. To enumerate a few of my particular beefs: I hate the way 'storied' is beginning to replace 'historic', and 'paraphrase' is used instead of 'adapt'; or 'fulsome' (which 'means' 'falsely over the top') is used to mean 'very full'. 'Beg the question' has long been a losing cause; it 'means' 'avoid the question by prejudging the answer', but – perhaps because 'beg' has some possible ambiguity to it – has come to mean 'ask the question'. I want British English to remain distinct from American English. I dislike the creeping use of 'out the door/window' rather than 'out of the door/window' (my old friend Ian McEwan used it thus in his latest novel *Lessons*, and when I queried it he replied, 'Oh, I like it, it just seems more concise'). Similarly, in sports commentary, American terms like 'an assist' or 'step up to the plate' are often now used, to no wiser purpose that I can see. And when someone a generation or two below me says: 'I like that you're here' instead of 'I'm glad that you're here', or 'I like the fact that you're here,' I tend to bridle. The construction – from German via American English – sounds wrong and harsh to my ear. And I have a visceral dislike of what has happened to the lovely word 'uxorious'; it used to describe a man who doted irredeemably on his wife; now it is applied to a man who has simply had a number of wives. I wouldn't call that uxoriousness, rather – at best – sentimental recidivism.

Or take that lovely, precise old verb 'to decimate'. From the Latin *decimare*, meaning to remove one tenth. As used of military punishments. When a Roman legion famously – or, should we say, infamously? – fought badly or behaved treasonably, the survivors were lined up and one in ten of them were killed. It was a terrible punishment but also a very precise one. Then slippage of meaning began, and nowadays the word is used as a synonym of massacre, wipe out, obliterate: in other words, kill more like nine out of ten. I know very good writers, even Professors of English, who misuse this term. You could say that they have decimated its meaning. Everyone seems out of step on this except me, and a handful of Latin scholars. And every time I see it used in this corrupt sense I feel what Evelyn Waugh once described as 'the senile itch to write letters to the newspapers'.

But if I were to use the word in its original, true sense, few would understand me. So the word has gone – or rather, its previous meaning has gone. As a writer, I acknowledge this without celebrating it; as a grumpy citizen, I repine. But as a former lexicographer, I look up the word's history in the OED and realize that this slippage of meaning, which I imagine to be of recent date, was in fact well under way during the nineteenth century. Language is tidal, oceanic, and the individual standing up with a placard of protest is inevitably washed away by a veritable tsunami . . . Hmm – 'tsunami'. Now don't get me started on *that*.

– Politics –

When I was a boy, my parents used to listen to *Any Questions?* on the wireless, as we then called it. I would sit through the programme in a state of consummate boredom, aware that this was grown-up business, and that the chance of there being a car-crash or a gunfight in it – apart from a metaphorical one – was non-existent. When I was a teenager, I would listen with a slightly larger understanding, though now with a kind of amazement that people could talk so fluently, know so much, argue so lucidly. A question would be proposed, answers would flow effortlessly from the panellists, applause would follow. Now, more than grown up, I sometimes watch *Question Time* on television with much the same mixture of appalled admiration. No one stops for breath, no one doubts. And most of all – I realise – no one ever changes their mind, or has their mind changed. No panellist is ever convinced by another's argument, no one ever says, 'Oh, now I see, of course you're right and I was wrong.' Opinions, whether expressed by a male or female panellist, are like virility symbols, not to be surrendered.

Some people are brought up in families where politics are openly and noisily discussed, and where tribalism is as deeply rooted as support for a football team. I grew up in the sort of quiet, middle-class English family in which politics, like religion and sex, were almost never mentioned. Not that my relatives didn't have political views. My maternal grandmother, for instance, was a Methodist who morphed into a socialist, and then a communist, and then – most original of all, especially in leafy Buckinghamshire – one who supported the Chinese rather than the Russians when the great Sino–Soviet split happened. Meanwhile, my grandfather was resolutely Tory. When I went to stay with them, Grandma would sit in her chair – in the red corner – tut-tutting over her *Daily Worker*, which exposed the fiendish iniquities of capitalism, while my grandfather sat in his chair – in the blue corner – reading the *Daily Express* and tut-tutting over the fiendish threats of Communism. But they never argued their views with one another – a truce had long since been called. As for my parents: my mother was, as she liked to put it, 'true blue', while my father's beliefs, as far as I could divine them, were more liberal. My brother used to be a theoretical anarchist 'of the Godwin/Spooner/Kropotkin sort', but tells me he hasn't thought about politics for decades, and hasn't voted in England since 1970.

I was slow to become interested in politics. I used to think: a plague on all your houses. I believed that the personal life and the artistic life were far more important than politics. Well, I still do believe that, just as strongly. I've never joined a political party, and have only marched in political rallies twice. But I've never not voted, and while I don't believe in making it compulsory, as in Australia, I think it's a personal as well as a civic duty. Even if you're voting against rather than for something.

During the sixty years I've had the franchise, I have voted, in local, parliamentary and European elections, for Labour, Conservative, Liberal, Liberal Democrat and Greens; also for the Women's Equality Party. I never contemplated voting for the SDP. I was once tempted in a local election to vote for a candidate whose name appeared at the very bottom of the list. This position had been achieved by changing their name to something beginning with Z, while the recently-invented party he or she was standing for was called 'None Of The Above'. But in the end this display of jaundiced wit didn't deflect me, and I voted for some of the usual suspects.

I haven't always owned up about my voting. I worked for the *New Statesman* in the late 1970s on the books and arts pages, and for more than a year didn't let on that in the previous general election I'd voted Liberal. When I finally confessed, my fellow-staffers treated my obvious simple-mindedness with surprising indulgence.

But though I've voted for six different parties in my life – and some independent candidates in local elections – I don't regard myself as ever having changed my mind. Or not much, anyway. It's the political parties which have changed, swerving this way and that, dodging for votes; I, the voter, have remained a man of principle. And I suspect many of us think like this. Oh, that was the year Labour went too far left for me to support them; or, that was the year the Tories went too far to the right. We keep the faith; it's the parties which are faithless, promiscuous, short-termist, shamelessly flexible of principle.

Some people, as they get older, become more conservative; over the years, among my friends and acquaintances, I've sometimes heard the familiar soft-shoe shuffle to the right. Those idealistic principles they had in their twenties have been rubbed away by exposure to the realities of life. Or, they've now got more money than they did and want to protect it, and hand it on. Or, they start hating young people's principles because they are remarkably similar to the ones they had in their own youth, principles they now realize are foolish delusions. Or, they simply don't want any more change in their lives, thank you very much. The European Referendum of 2016 offered a departure from this last notion. While three-quarters of young people voted to Remain in the European Union, two-thirds of older people voted to leave – which would result in considerable change to their lives. Though it's also true that voting to leave – given the identity of its leading campaigners – represented a move to the right.

Then there's the Never Again factor, which applies both to parties and their leaders. No, I couldn't possibly vote for . . . and then fill in the name of the party leader, be it Tony Blair or Michael Howard or Nick Clegg. The single time I voted Conservative was when the two main parties were led respectively by Harold Wilson and Edward Heath. This would have been the election of 1974. Heath, much mocked for his wooden manner, was a liberal, pro-European, unposh Tory, who had booted Enoch Powell out of the cabinet and called Robert Maxwell 'the unacceptable face of capitalism'. He was also the only Prime Minister to have fought in the Second World War, and had therefore witnessed the consequences of European schisms. Wilson, even by the standards of politics, seemed to me – and still does – less than scrupulous: deviously shifting his party this way and that for short-term advantage, anti- or pro-European according to his parliamentary needs. And so that time I favoured Heath's Conservative Party. My single vote, powerful though it was, couldn't alas prevent Wilson from securing victory.

Similarly, in 1997, when I voted for Tony Blair's Labour Party, this was mainly because it was necessary to evict the Tories. I'd interviewed Blair for the *New Yorker* magazine when he became leader of the Party, and hadn't found him at all left-wing. I expected him, if he came to power, to be a kind of decent Tory. My old friend Anthony Howard, former editor of the *New Statesman,* liked to refer to him as 'Little Boy Blue'. And so he proved. After 1997, I went back to voting for the Liberal Democrats, who seemed, indeed were, to the left of the Blairite Labour Party. I remember especially Charles Kennedy's stand against the Iraq War. True, in this period the Lib Dems seemed to change their leader as often as their underclothes, but like many I assumed their essential principles remained the same. I failed to notice the rise of the Orange Book tendency, so in the run-up to the 2010 Election, I assumed that if there was going to be a coalition, it would be a Lib-Lab pact. And then it very much wasn't, and then the Lib Dems went back en masse on their pre-election pledge about university tuition fees, and that was the end of them for me. So Never Again.

When I look back at the innumerable conversations I've had with friends and colleagues about political matters over the decades, I can't remember a single, clear instance, when a single, clear argument has made me change my mind – or when I have changed someone else's mind. Such conversations seem to consist of one person stating their position or prejudice, with supporting factual documentation, before another person does the same, but with an opposite conclusion.

Occasionally, there might be an area where you admit to knowing little, and are a vessel waiting to be filled. But such moments are rare. In other words, private political arguments are dismayingly closer to those of *Any Questions?* and *Question Time* than I would like to admit – even if less articulate.

So am I saying that, despite all my zig-zags, I have never changed my political mind? Well, sort of, yes. I'm not claiming this as a virtue, particularly. It may be stubbornness, or laziness. If Maynard Keynes changed his mind when the facts changed, I find that facts and events tend to confirm me in what I already believe. But another thing has been going on in my lifetime: the centre ground of politics has moved to the right. Mrs Thatcher, once asked what her greatest success had been, replied killingly, 'Tony Blair.' Whereas there had previously been little pendulum swings to the left and then the right as Labour and Conservatives swapped power, Mrs Thatcher rehung the whole clock at a different angle on the wall. And so, by staying still, someone of my political beliefs has found himself moving further to the left as the centre moved away from him. Whereas forty or so years ago, I might have seemed a right-wing Labourite, or perhaps a left-wing Tory – or, indeed, the capital-L Liberal that I sometimes was – now I probably sound like a Corbynista. Indeed, I continued to vote Labour under Corbyn's leadership in the 2019 Election, despite my dismay at his vapid performance during the European Referendum. But that is one of the functions of politicians – to disappoint us.

The historian A. J. P. Taylor, applying for a fellowship at Oxford, was asked an anxious question by one of the dons interviewing him. He had heard that Mr Taylor regrettably suffered from a dubious condition known as Strong Opinions: was this the case? Yes, Taylor confirmed, he did indeed have Strong Opinions, but it was all right, because they were Weakly Held. (And he got the job.) Some of us have strong opinions weakly held, others weak opinions strongly held. I've always assumed that liberals like me have moderate opinions, moderately held. But I'm not sure that's any longer the case. When asked my view on some public matter nowadays, I tend to reply, 'Well, in Barnes's Benign Republic . . .'. The other day a friend asked for details of the BBR's main principles. For a start, I replied, public ownership of all forms of mass transport, and all forms of power supply – gas, electric, nuclear, wind, solar. Major reform of the House of Lords, which has weirdly engrossed itself into the second largest legislative body in the world, second only to the national congress of the Chinese Communist Party; also, with its twenty-six bishops, the only chamber to have theological input apart from Iran (and if reform doesn't work, then Abolition). A referendum on the future of the monarchy, which I would expect monarchists to win; but after that, and in any case, the institution would have to become self-funding and fully taxable, with absolute financial transparency (no more bags of cash for the King's private charities) and no government support. Immediate application to rejoin the European Union; permission for Scotland to hold another independence referendum if they want to; encouragement for the island of Ireland to reunite. Massive investment in the National Health Service on both moral and economic grounds; the market to be completely removed from the NHS, and foreign health-care companies banned from buying up GP practices. Immediate unilateral nuclear disarmament, plus a dismantling of the arms industry; no export of arms would be permitted, and only the manufacture of those necessary for the country's defence. Absolute commitment to carbon net zero sooner than other countries. A ban on any foreign country or institution or individual from owning any newspaper or television station, or any sporting institution, in the BBR.

And yes, there's more. Absolute separation of Church and State, and the laicisation of all education. Immediate abolition of the charitable status of public schools; then, in stage two, abolition of the schools themselves. A fifty-year ban on any Old Etonian from becoming Prime Minister; a twenty-five-year ban on one becoming a cabinet minister. A complete prohibition on foreign missionaries entering the country; and a ban on domestic missionaries travelling overseas. Responsibility for the prison services to be returned to the state. Immediate legalisation on assisted dying. Universal right to roam on public land, greater access to private land for walkers and ramblers. All major sporting events (as defined by me) will be returned to free-to-air TV channels and websites. Anonymity on social media will be banned: all contributors to be immediately identifiable, which might reduce the insane level of verbal violence, and make it easier to identify and prosecute criminal posters. Full restoration of all arts and humanities courses at schools and universities (every child must learn a minimum of one foreign language); and, more widely, an end to a purely utilitarian view of education. At least one of the royal palaces to be turned into a museum of the slave trade, with full explanations of its profitability and beneficiaries. Education (and re-education, and re-re-education) of young males to diminish violence against and coercion of women. Oh, and while we're about it, I think we'd better just close down the *Daily Mail,* don't you?

Inevitably, such measures would be denounced by 'those who know better', who 'understand the real world' as unaffordable, untested, absurdly utopian, blindly socialistic, certain to cause a disastrous run on the pound, and so on. 'Not even Liz Truss, whose seven-week premiership cost the country thirty billion pounds . . .' op-ed columns might begin (if they didn't prefer to ignore such blatant lunacy). Whereas I consider these proposals to be reasonable, gentle and quite possibly popular. 'Ah, but the markets won't stand for any of it . . . '. No, they probably wouldn't. But a spokesman for the BBR (me) will reply by quoting Charles de Gaulle. When he was president, a particular policy was put forward at his council of ministers. No, no, replied some of his more cautious and traditional advisors, we can't possibly do that, it will cause a run on the Franc – the markets won't stand for it. To which the General replied, with an hauteur appropriate to one of his height, 'The policy of La France is not made on the trading floor of the Bourse.'

'You don't make the poor richer by making the rich poorer,' Mrs Thatcher used to declare in her patronisingly oleaginous tone. Whenever she said that, I used to think, Well, it sounds like a pretty good idea to me, why not give it a try? Under her premiership, the differential between rich and poor reverted to levels not seen since Victorian times; and that gap has continued to widen. Equally spurious is the often-quoted theory of 'trickle-down economics', whereby some of the wealth of the rich will inevitably find its way to the poor as the rich spend their money in shops, create jobs and so on. But it always seemed to me that the down-pipe was blocked. John Major once said he wanted wealth not just to trickle, but to 'cascade down the generations'; but in reality it has continued to cascade largely down the generations of the already rich.

And will all this, Monsieur le Président Barnes, result in a Peaceable Kingdom in England's green and pleasant land, where the lion will lie down with the lamb? No – utopias by their very name and nature do not exist. But it might be a damn sight kinder and nicer place to live in. Also, writing all this out, I realise I've changed my mind: I do have Strong Opinions, and they are Strongly Held.

– Books –

If reading is one of the pleasures – and necessities – of youth, rereading is one of the pleasures – and necessities – of age. You know more, you understand both life and literature better, and you have the additional interest of checking your younger self against your older self. Occasionally I will reread a book in exactly the same copy as I first did decades previously: and there, in, say, a student text of a Flaubert novel, I will find all those annotations which now, initially, embarrass. Key passages underlined, exclamations in the margin of 'Irony!' or 'Symbol!' or 'Repeated image!' and so on. And yet often, naive and excited as they seem, these comments are pretty much ones I might be making – if not so explicitly – several decades on. That younger reader wasn't wrong: it *was* ironic, it *was* symbolic, it *was* a repeated image. I don't think you are a more intelligent reader at sixty-five than at twenty-five; just a more subtle one, and better able to make comparisons with other books and other writers, set against the extra knowledge of extra life.

Sometimes you change your mind about a writer. Perhaps, when you first read them you were only pretending to admire what you'd been told to admire. But also your tastes change. For instance, at twenty-five I was more open to writers telling me how to live and how to think; by forty-five I had come to dislike didacticism. I don't want to be told how to think and how to live by, say, Bernard Shaw, or D. H. Lawrence or Sir David Hare or the later Tolstoy. I don't like art – especially theatrical art – whose function appears to challenge, yet ends up reassuring us that we are on the right side. Sitting there complacently agreeing with a playwright that war is bad, that capitalism is bad, that bad people are bad. 'You don't make art out of good intentions,' is one of Flaubert's wiser pronouncements.

Sometimes, when our tastes become more defined, they become narrower: we grow out of some writers who adorned our youth. But this doesn't have to be the case. When I was young, I read quite a lot of detective fiction, including Simenon's Maigret novels. I enjoyed them in both English and French (the latter aided by the novelist's restricted vocabulary of only about 2,000 words).

Gradually, I learned a little about his life – his great fame and wealth, his frenetic womanising and sexual boastfulness, and the extraordinary belief that he ought to win the Nobel Prize. Annually, he would denounce the 'cretins' of Stockholm who had given the Prize to someone else. Then, one day, I asked my friend Anita Brookner what she was currently reading, and to my surprise she replied 'Simenon'. Not the Maigrets (of which there are about seventy-five) but the *romans durs* (of which there are around 200). Would she recommend one in particular? *Chez Krull*, she replied. I bought a copy, but only read a few pages. Some years later, when Anita died, I decided to read the novel in tribute to her. And began to discover a new, deeper, darker Simenon, one in which the world is not discovered and explained to you by a companionable detective, but put there, unmediated, in front of you, without judgement, in all its bleakness and moral ambiguity. And I discovered a great writer, one lauded by Faulkner, Gide (both of them Nobellists), Colette, Francois Mauriac, Muriel Spark, T. S. Eliot, Somerset Maugham, John le Carré and many others. Gide called him 'the greatest of all, the most genuine novelist we have had in literature'. In January 1948, when he was seventy-eight, he wrote in his journal, 'New plunge into Simenon; I have just read six in a row.' A few days later, he notes, 'He makes one reflect; and this is close to being the height of art; how superior he is to those heavy novelists who do not spare us a single commentary!' Recently, I found myself – at much the same age as Gide – 'plunging' similarly, into even more than six in a row. And yes, I do now believe he should have won the Nobel Prize.

Then there is a rarer changing of the mind, which is even more enriching: when a writer to whom you had previously been indifferent, indeed almost despised, suddenly makes sense to you, and you realize, with, yes, a kind of joy, that at last you have seen the point of them. I first read E. M. Forster when an English master handed out a list of Great Books to be read one summer holiday. *A Passage to India* was on that list. I still have the orange Penguin edition – a reprint of 1960, price three shillings and sixpence – in which I read the novel. There are no notes in the margin, not a single cry of 'Irony!' It clearly made little impression on me; or rather, I didn't know what to think about the book's main themes. Later, of my own volition, when I was about twenty, I read *A Room With a View,* and actively began to take against Forster.

This short novel seemed to me a fusty, musty, dusty read, with rather antique prose and a storyline and characters which failed to engage me. The English novelists of the next generation – Huxley, Waugh, Greene – spoke to me with much more clarity and purpose.

What often happens, when you decide against a writer, is that everything thereafter tends to confirm that prejudice. I read parts of Forster's *Aspects of the Novel* and discovered his famous dictum that, 'Yes – oh dear yes – the novel tells a story . . . and I wish that it was not so.' This struck me as exceedingly . . . feeble. Of course the novel tells a story, I thought, and if you aren't up to telling a story, why write a novel? And indeed Forster had stopped writing fiction at forty-five, then lived on for another forty-six years, in the process becoming a grander and grander (if still modest) old man. Nowadays, I would admire a writer who falls silent because he or she has nothing more to say; in my youth, I was less forgiving.

And then there was that other Forsterian dictum: 'If I had to choose between betraying my country and betraying my friend, I hope I should have the guts to betray my country.' This may sound fine in theoretical, high-minded Bloomsburyite discussions, in which the personal life is held of greater value than the public life. But try telling that to, for instance, the families of those betrayed by Kim Philby. How many deaths was he responsible for? Forty or fifty, perhaps. Rather more consequential than just doing the dirty on a chum.

But there was a final, and barely sensible – but to me very powerful – reason for cold-shouldering Forster. I was and remain a great admirer of Ford Madox Ford. He was a rare English fictional modernist, with two masterpieces – *The Good Soldier* and *Parade's End* – to his credit, and at least a half a dozen more very interesting books; under-appreciated when he was writing, and only a little less so nowadays. Forster and Ford met at a country-house weekend in the summer of 1914, at which Ford seems to have been the only person present clearly able to see that war was inevitable.

Afterwards, Forster snootily noted in his diary that Ford was 'rather a fly-blown man of letters'. That was a bad call. And then there was the fact that, every time I went into a bookshop, new or secondhand, and looked to see what they had by Ford Madox Ford, he would be crowded out by the alphabetical proximity of shelf-yards of E. M.

Bloody Forster. And, just to show that I wasn't merely mad, I had another go at *A Room With a View* in my forties. No, it still didn't cut the mustard. And that, seemingly, was that.

So what made me change my mind? It began from a quite unexpected source, an anthology of food writing. There I came across Forster's description of the breakfast he was served on an early-morning boat train to London in the 1930s:

'Porridge or prunes, sir?' That cry still rings in my memory. It is an epitome – not, indeed, of English food, but of the forces that drag it into the dirt. It voices the true spirit of gastronomic joylessness. Porridge fills the Englishman up, prunes clear him out, so their functions are opposed. But their spirit is the same: they eschew pleasure and consider delicacy immoral . . . Everything was grey. The porridge was in grey lumps, the prunes swam in grey sauce . . . Then I had a haddock. It was covered in a sort of hard, yellow oilskin, as if it had been in a lifeboat, and its inside gushed salt water when pricked. Sausages and bacon followed this disgusting fish. They, too, had been up all night. Toast like steel: marmalade a scented jelly. I paid the bill dumbly, wondering again why some things have to be. They have to be because this is England, and we are English.

This wasn't at all like my long-formed picture of the novelist: it was funny, subversive, delightfully unpatriotic, and all too true by the sound of it. But this might just have been a moment of aberration, I assumed, an atypical swerve into humour. What finally did the trick was just as left-field, a conversation I had a few years later with a friend about opera. In my sixties I belatedly fell in love with opera, and we were discussing its representation in fiction. 'Oh,' she said, 'and there's that scene in a provincial Italian opera house in *Where Angels Fear to Tread*.' Forster's first novel, published in 1905. Not one I'd tried and failed with before. It looked agreeably short. And then it surprised me from the very first chapter: it was swift, witty and satirical, with a fine eye for English manners and English snobbery. Here are a couple of lines conveying the essence of the starchy, stuck-up Harriet:

'Harriet, though she did not care for music, knew how to listen to it.'

and

'Everyone to his taste!' said Harriet, who always delivered a platitude as if it was an epigram.

The opera-house scene, when I got to it, was brilliant. The work being performed is *Lucia di Lammermoor,* a knowing nod to the same opera's famous appearance in *Madame Bovary.* This in itself showed spirit, if not recklessness: a first novelist, five years into the twentieth century, taking on one of the great scenes of the greatest nineteenth-century novel. And yet Forster emerges unharmed by the comparison. His opera scene is his own. The production of *Lucia* is camply bad; the local audience riotously over-relaxed; the English visitors embarrassed and stuffily disapproving. It could have been just coarsely satirical and humanly disparaging; instead, the tone − of ironical amusement at the cheerful follies of the world − is perfectly pitched. And the scene also contains the following lines, which had me reaching for my annotating pencil:

There is something majestic in the bad taste of Italy; it is not the bad taste of a country which knows no better; it has not the nervous vulgarity of England, or the blinded vulgarity of Germany. It observes beauty, and chooses to pass it by. But it attains to beauty's confidence.

Where was that fusty, musty, dusty writer I had

imagined Forster to be? Nowhere at all in this first novel of his. Next I read *Howards End,* and finally realized what a grown-up novelist Forster is; how serious his concerns; how good he is on marriage, friendship, love and hopeless desire; how well he writes about women; on the choice between art and life, art and money, taste and vulgarity; how well he understands the power of convention and the unheroic but necessary journeys a life entails; how wry and sly he can be, and yet how powerfully reflective. Perhaps I had mistaken his manner, or been expecting something he wasn't offering; though most likely, I hadn't known enough about life to appreciate him.

I read on, with *The Longest Journey* – publicly, his least successful novel, and yet his own favourite. There I discovered a writer who was also formally audacious in a way I would never have anticipated: in his handling of time; in the way he gives us a protagonist's back-story audaciously late in the day; and in his killing-off of characters just as we assume they are about to become important. One reviewer calculated that – infants excepted – more than forty-four per cent of the adult population of this novel fall beneath the author's capricious sword.

I don't regret my decades of failing to appre-

ciate Forster. Rereading would be a dull and com-
placent business if it always resulted in a simple
confirmation of what you had previously thought.
And the pleasure of being proved wrong can be
a genuine pleasure. But as you may imagine, this
experience has made me reconsider some other
speedy judgements of my youth. Who else might
I have to change my mind about? Hmm. Anthony
Powell? Saul Bellow? Iris Murdoch? Actually,
despite what I said earlier, I've recently been reading some of D. H. Lawrence's short fiction recently,
and I'm beginning to think I might – just possibly –
be wrong about him too.

– Age and Time –

(B)ut first, a pause, and a parenthesis. Rereading this essay, I am struck less by the frank admission of ways in which I have changed my mind, as by an underlying resistance to admitting that I have done so. I think this is a common trait. We may admit to two or three major shifts in our lifetime – which we would have to be blind not to see – but on the whole prefer to believe that we are consistent human beings rather than seaweed tossed around by the tides. We believe – we have to believe, otherwise we would be lost – in the integrity of the personality; also in the continuity of our lives making narrative sense. We don't like to think we have lost the plot. So, for instance, when writing about politics, I attributed my peripatetic voting habits to my own consistency, and the febrility of the political parties out for my support. But a more objective examiner might detect a weakness of principle – or basic lack of sufficient interest – in my divagations. I might sound like the proud mother watching her son's regiment march past and observing, 'They're all out of step except our Jack.'

So, to put it the other way round, what can I say, with any moderate degree of certainty, that I *haven't* changed my mind about in the course of my adult life?

– the primacy of love.

– the primacy of art, and the belief that literature is the best system we have of understanding the world.

– the certainty that death leads to absolute and eternal oblivion.

– the certainty that religion – all religions – are at best comforting fantasies, whose antiquity and rituals, plus violent threats, seek to persuade us of their truth (and at worst, as Lucretius put it centuries ago, *tantum religio potuit suadere malorum* – 'So powerful is religion in inducing us to evil acts'). Even if it must be hard to admit that what your ancestors believed for generation upon generation, and went to their deaths believing, is bunkum.

– that the irreligious are just as moral (or immoral) as the religious; perhaps more so, as they have worked out their morality for themselves.

– that, *pace* Mrs Thatcher, there is such a thing as society.

– that scientific and technological inventions – the railways, the internet, AI – are morally neutral, capable of bringing both social benefit and social harm. The idea that they have some innate moral value is delusional.

– that self-interest will generally outweigh altruism.

– that I am either a cheerful pessimist or a melancholy optimist, depending on which side of the bed I get out of.

And finally:

– that there is great joy – undiminishing joy, joy to last a lifetime – in sport, plus even a certain amount of moral value.)

One afternoon in January 2016, I went to see Dora, who has cut my hair in North London for about twenty years. As I settled into the chair, damp and dripping, I said, 'Now I want your best shot, Dora, because I've got a Big Birthday coming up.'

'Well, you know what they say, Julian,' she replied sweetly, 'Sixty is the new forty.' Which was kind of her, but as I explained, 'Unfortunately, seventy is the new sixty-eight.'

We live inside time; it surrounds us and holds

us; it marks our beginnings and our ends; it dates our favourite moments and our blackest days; we refer to it all the . . . time – well, there you go. But though it's ever-present in our lives, we don't think about it very much. It's hard for our minds – especially for pragmatic British minds – to deal with abstraction in the first place, let alone such an abstraction as time. And when physicists tell us strange, unaccountable new facts and theories about how it might bend and double back on itself, or exist in parallel realities, I suspect that most of us throw up our hands. There are the things scientists tell us about the essential nature of life and time and space, which we acknowledge as doubtless being the case; and then there are the domestic, old-fashioned analogue assumptions we fall back on and which rule our lives.

Mostly, we live as stumbling amateurs in a largely incomprehensible professional universe. Albert Einstein was once asked to explain relativity in a way that even journalists could understand. 'An hour sitting with a pretty girl on a park bench passes like a minute,' he said. 'But a minute sitting on a hot stove seems like an hour. That's relativity.' This may seem clear and funny enough, but I'm not sure I'm any closer to understanding the Special or General Theories of Relativity.

I think it's largely true that we conflate abstract time with pragmatic age. Also, that our sense of time is slow to develop. As I child, I think I experienced time more as a question of speed. Life had two essential speeds, non-existent and slow. You didn't even notice it when you were playing a game, reading a book, inspecting an exotic animal at the zoo, watching a steam train pass, eating an ice-cream. Those moments were entire of themselves, context-free, absolute. And then, for much of the rest of childhood, there was slowness: those long, elastic spans when you were waiting for the next thing to happen – for a birthday, for Christmas, for fireworks to be let off, for conkers to patter down from horse-chestnut trees. 'Are we there yet?' is the symbolic cry of childhood. What we are waiting for, impatiently, is adulthood. Philip Larkin wrote of his childhood as 'a forgotten boredom'. I don't think I was bored as a child. That state began later: and my adolesecence is a pretty well-remembered boredom. One advantage of being adult is that boredom now is as nothing compared to the boredom of childhood and youth.

As a child, I didn't think about how age and time worked for adults. There seemed to be only two sorts of adults: those of your parents' generation, and the others beyond it, old if not very old people, all cardigans and whiskers and deaf-aids. Adulthood appeared to be a condition as solid as it was unattainable. It felt as if adults understood everything – except, perhaps, children – and that their world was stable. It never occurred to me that adults might be faking things, either in their reactions or their expressed feelings, or in their very comprehension of life. Insofar as I thought about it, I assumed that for them, time must run as stably as their lives seemed to run. Then I grew up, and changed my mind: I realised that adulthood is not at all as solid and stolid as it looked from the outside, and that all its supposed certainties were liable to deliquesce at any moment.

What deceives the child, understandably so, is that the life ahead seems to be predictably marked out by a series of dates and ages at which things are supposed to happen. Loss of milk teeth, long trousers, first menstruation, the age at which you transfer from one school to another, the age at which it is legal to have sex, to vote, to enlist and die for your country. Twenty-one, key to the door, as it used to be said. Followed by the various reliable stages of adulthood until, at sixty or sixty-five, comes your pension, which can also be relied upon, unless it has mysteriously disappeared under the stewardship of Robert Maxwell or Philip Green.

The child distinguishes rigorously, and proudly, between being six-and-a-half and six-and three-quarters. The adult takes the longer view, marking things out by decades; and all through the process of living there are comforting wise saws and modern instances to fall back on. For example: 'You're only as old as you feel.' I've never thought there was much truth in that. It seems in part a wilful denial of death; also, an invitation to embarrassing skittishness. I think, as a sceptical realist, that you are precisely as old as your driving licence and passport insist you are, and that you shouldn't pretend otherwise. Then there's 'You're only as old as you look.' George Orwell ruefully laid it down that, 'At fifty, everyone has the face he deserves.' He himself didn't live to find out whether or not this applied to him – he died at forty-six; but in any case I don't think this much-quoted dictum is true either. Rather, it's an expression of Orwell's innate puritanism. Genes are far more important than merit when it comes to aging. We can all think of people of fifty who look much younger than that. And I'm not talking about those who've had a little nip and tuck, a bit of filler here and botox there. In my – perhaps jaundiced – opinion, there's nothing more aging than a face-lift.

As for time, one of the discoveries of adulthood is that, far from it running more smoothly, as the child imagines, there are frequent hiccuping gear-changes. Edith Wharton wrote that, 'Time, when it is left to itself and no definite demands are made of it, cannot be trusted to move at any recognised pace. Usually it loiters, but just when one has come to count upon its slowness, it may suddenly break into a wild irrational gallop.' This is truest at times of deepest emotion: for instance, love and grief.

Love is often seen as an experience in which the normal rules of the universe no longer apply. The poet Louis MacNeice famously wrote: 'Time was away and somewhere else.' Physical laws, from gravity to entropy, seem to be suspended without our even noticing, and the world is reduced to a reflection in the lover's eye.

I think this is probably truer of sexual passion than of love itself. In my experience love produces a change in our sense of time which is more para-doxical than this. On the one hand, yes, we want time to stand still, to be 'away and somewhere else' – and we want that moment to last forever. This might be ascribed to our poetic side. But we also have a prose side. And it is this prose side which wants time to roll on in its usual way, if not indeed faster, because it is only time that will confirm this love to be real and substantial rather than a passing delusion. The suspension of time might identify love, but the active presence of time is necessary to verify it. So we want both an eternal now, and an urgent future. A vivid present, but also a looking forward to the time when we can begin to look back.

As for grief, which marks the physical, though not the emotional, ending of love, that too messes with our sense of time. Grief is both a state and a process. Nowadays we put our emphasis far too much on it being a process: something to be gone through, got over, so that we may, in that dreadful and dishonest modern banality, be able to 'move on'. This is partly because in a post-religious society we turn our backs on death, foolishly treating it as a problem that can be solved, can be rationalised away; it's also a pragmatic selfishness. A friend of mine was sitting at her desk in a newspaper office, weeping at the loss of her father. Her boss came past and asked what was the matter. She explained that her father had died six weeks previously. 'Oh,

I thought you'd be over that by now,' he replied. Deal with it; move on. Except that grief, as I said, is a state as well as a process. And as with love, time simultaneously both stops and moves. You want it to stop – to be a state, so that you can hold on as much as possible to the image and the memory of the lost loved one; but you also want it to be a process, one which will convey you out of this strange new land of pain before your spirit breaks.

And then there is death itself. Now in my late seventies, I have inevitably experienced quite a number of deaths of those near to me; nowadays, with my closest friends, there is often a moment when we wonder – sometimes quite openly – which of us will be going to the other one's funeral. But first there is the dying to be got through. Being with someone to whom medical science has given the thumbs-down thrusts us into a spin-drier of emotion. There are things to be said, and things not to be said; questions to be asked, and questions to be suppressed. One thing I've never been able to ask – not that I've thought about asking it till now – is whether the dying person's sense of time is affected. You would expect it to be. On the one hand, there is the hourly, daily emphasis on keeping alive and being kept alive, full of pulse-taking and blood-taking and pill-taking, and regular time-keeping; on the other hand, there is what awaits rushingly ahead, an eternity of nothingness, a place where time will indeed be 'away and somewhere else' in the worst, most extreme fashion. Does this skew our sense of time in those last weeks and months? 'Well, we shall find out,' as Larkin put it. I shall certainly be interested in the answer – assuming I have time to reflect on my own dying, which can't ever be guaranteed. But who knows, perhaps a friendly radio producer with a microphone will come along to my bedside, and ask the right questions. If so, I'll be able to let you know.